Contents

What are towns and cities?

Towns and cities are places where people live. Each one is home to thousands of people. Most contain services such as shops, supermarkets, banks, leisure centres and railway stations. Cities are usually bigger than towns. They often have extra services such as **universities** and airports.

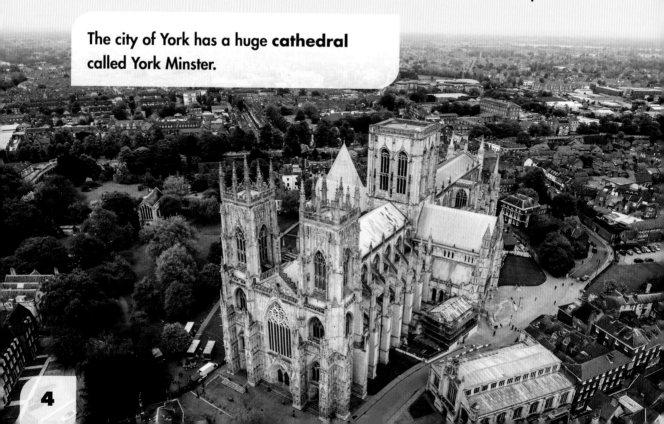

The city of York has a huge **cathedral** called York Minster.

LET'S EXPLORE BRITAIN

Villages, Towns and Cities

JAMES NIXON

a Capstone company — publishers for children

Raintree is an imprint of Capstone Global Library Limited, a company incorporated in England and Wales having its registered office at 264 Banbury Road, Oxford, OX2 7DY – Registered company number: 6695582

www.raintree.co.uk
myorders@raintree.co.uk

Edited by James Nixon
Designed by Keith Williams, sprout.uk.com
Picture Research by James Nixon
Production by Discovery Books
Originated by Capstone Global Library Limited
Printed and bound in China

ISBN 978 1 4747 5900 7
22 21 20 19 18
10 9 8 7 6 5 4 3 2 1

British Library Cataloguing in Publication Data
A full catalogue record for this book is available from the British Library.

Acknowledgements
We would like to thank the following for permission to reproduce photographs:
Cover Image (Andrei Nekrassov/Shutterstock); Alamy: pp. 14 (Robin Weaver), 18 (Julian Eales), 19 (Ian Miles-Flashpoint Pictures), 21 (Tracey Whitefoot), 22 (Doug Houghton SCO), 23 (Colin Palmer Photography), 28 (Patrick Nairne), 29 (Ian Canham); Shutterstock: pp. 4 (Christoph Lischetzki), 5 (BasPhoto), 6 (antb), 7 (Caron Badkin), 8 (Prakich Treetasayuth), 9 (PhotoLondonUK), 10 (peresanz), 11 (S.Borisov), 12 (Lois GoBe), 13 (Kanuman), 15 (PhotoLondonUK), 16 (Jacek Wojnarowski), 17 (pcruciatti), 20 (Milosz Maslanka), 24 (Kevin Eaves), 25 (Oscar Johns), 26 (Jeanette Teare), 27 (jax10289).

We would like to thank Dr Gillian Fyfe for her invaluable help in the preparation of this book.

Long ago, places were called cities if they contained a cathedral. Today, the Queen can name other large and important towns as cities. There are 60 cities across the UK. Not all cities are big. St Davids in Wales has a cathedral but a **population** of less than 2,000 people.

Reading is the largest town in the UK that is not a city. Over 230,000 people live there.

What is a village?

Villages are usually smaller than towns. They are surrounded by countryside. **Populations** of villages range from a few hundred to a few thousand people. Places without a church and just a few houses are called **hamlets**. Villages have fewer services than a town. But some may have a pub, a post office or even a doctor's surgery.

Corton Denham in Somerset has a population of less than 200.

Villages developed as homes for **rural** workers, such as farmers, fishermen and miners. Over the years, some villages have become smaller because people have moved away. Other villages have grown much larger to **merge** with towns. Many buildings in villages are old. Houses may have stone walls, wooden beams or thatched roofs.

Some of the houses with black wooden beams in Weobley, Herefordshire, were built in **medieval** times.

How did settlements develop?

Many centuries ago, the first **settlements** were built on flat, dry land next to farmland. It was also ideal to build a settlement near a river. Settlers used the river's water for drinking, washing and watering crops. Rivers were also good for transport. People and goods could travel on rivers by boat.

The town of Knaresborough in North Yorkshire was built by the River Nidd.

Large towns called **ports** grew on the coast or by rivers that led out to sea. Factories and **industries** were set up at ports because ships could travel there. Some cities have grown because industries, such as coal, steel or cotton, provided huge numbers of jobs.

Liverpool is one of Britain's biggest ports. Nearly half a million people live there.

Capital cities

A capital is the most important city in a country. The leaders of a country work in the capital. London is the UK's capital city. It was built on the River Thames by the **Romans** around 2,000 years ago. They called it Londinium. Today, London is a huge **port** with a **population** of around 9 million people.

"Gherkin"

London's skyline has many impressive buildings including the oval-shaped "Gherkin".

Large capital cities such as London have many famous **landmarks**. Buckingham Palace is the home of the Queen. The country's laws are made at the Houses of Parliament. London is a world-famous city. It receives more than 20 million **tourists** every year.

A tall clock tower nicknamed Big Ben stands at one end of the Houses of Parliament.

Each nation that makes up the UK has its own capital city. The port of Cardiff is the capital of Wales. It grew rapidly in the 1800s, when ships carried coal from there around the world. Northern Ireland's capital is Belfast. Belfast is a port that once had one of the largest shipbuilding industries in the world. The passenger ship SS *Titanic* was built in Belfast.

Today, Cardiff Bay is now busy with shops, restaurants and cafés.

Glasgow is Scotland's biggest city. But the capital of Scotland is Edinburgh. This is where the Scottish government makes its laws. Edinburgh is the UK's second most popular destination for tourists. Visitors flock to Edinburgh to look at the old buildings or watch some of the city's famous arts **festivals**.

Edinburgh Castle perches on top of a rocky crag.

City features

Cities and large towns provide lots of jobs. They have huge office blocks and large factories. People love to shop in cities. Many cities have big indoor shopping centres. These contain popular **chain stores**. Chain stores are shops that can be found in towns and cities all over the country.

Town centres in major cities are often **pedestrianised**. This means that people can shop safely.

Bullring Shopping Centre, Birmingham

In the biggest cities, you can see **skyscrapers** and gigantic sports stadiums. The roads get very busy. Cities have transport systems to help people move around. London has an underground train network called the Tube. Other cities have tracks for **trams**.

Old Trafford in Manchester is the second largest football stadium in Britain. Wembley in London is the biggest stadium.

Living in the city

Cities contain many different types of houses. **Inner cities** are close to the city centre and are more crowded. Here, many people live in **flats**, tower blocks and terraced houses. Terraces are rows of houses that are joined together. In the **suburbs**, streets are less busy and crowded. Houses are often **detached** with large gardens.

Hundreds of terraced houses line the streets in the city of Bristol.

Living in the city has many advantages. There are offices, shops and lots of entertainments nearby. Cities have sporting events, cinemas, museums, art galleries and much more to see and do. It is easy for people to use buses, taxis and other transport. However, traffic jams are common. The amount of traffic can cause **pollution**.

There is lots of entertainment at night in cities.

New towns

In World War II (1939–1945), many people's homes were destroyed by German bombs. By the end of the war, there was a shortage of houses. Some cities, such as London and Glasgow, had also got too crowded. Many people lived in poor housing called **slums**. To solve these problems, **new towns** were built outside the cities.

Stevenage became Britain's first new town in 1946.

In the 1960s, many more homes were built. Telford was a new town west of Birmingham. Old towns, such as Northampton, were made much larger. Outside Liverpool, the towns of Warrington and Runcorn grew in size. Milton Keynes is a famous new town. In 1967, it was just a village. Now it has a **population** of over 200,000.

Town planners laid out Milton Keynes' roads like a grid.

Market towns

Many of Britain's old towns developed as market towns. These towns were given the right to hold markets many centuries ago. Markets were held on certain days of the week. Farmers, butchers, craftspeople and other **traders** came to the market to sell their goods. People visited the market to chat to each other as well as trade.

Cirencester in Gloucestershire is one of Britain's oldest market towns.

Other places near to a market town were not allowed to hold their own markets. This meant that markets attracted people from a wide area. As the markets got busier, the towns grew bigger. Lots of market towns still hold markets today.

A market is held on five days of the week in Newark-on-Trent, Nottinghamshire.

Inside towns and villages

In a town centre, you will find a main street lined with shops. This is called the **high street**. Market towns have a market square where traders set up their stalls. The town may also have a market cross. These stone structures mark where markets are held. Some towns have a large town hall where public meetings take place.

A market cross stands in the Scottish town of Jedburgh.

The main feature of a village is the church. Some churches have huge towers, or spires. A village green is a grassy area in the middle of a village. On the village green, villagers can hold fairs and other celebrations. Many villages have a pond where you can feed the ducks.

A village green and duck pond in Finchingfield, Essex.

23

Living in a village

There are few jobs and services in villages. People have to travel further to work and shop. There is often little or no public transport. In **remote** parts of Britain, villages can be many miles from the nearest town. Car journeys often have to be made on narrow, winding roads.

Remote villages in the mountains can be cut off by snow.

Chapel Stile, Lake District

However, there are many good things about living in a village. There is more space. There is also less **pollution** and noise. People can enjoy the beautiful and peaceful countryside. In villages, people often know each other. Churches, pubs and village fêtes give people the chance to get to know one another better.

Children enjoy a maypole dance at a village **carnival** in Ashover, Derbyshire.

How are places changing?

Cities and towns are always changing. **Inner cities** sometimes have **abandoned** factories and run-down housing. These can be knocked down and replaced with smart new developments. This is called **regeneration**.

Sheffield's city centre has been regenerated. It has a huge glasshouse called the Winter Garden. It contains plants from around the world.

Towns and cities grow when new houses are built. **Retail parks** with shops are also built on the edges of towns. This is because it is cheaper to build outside of the town or city centre. There is more space here and parking is easier. People are shopping less in town centres than they used to. Some shops in town centres have closed down.

A typical retail park outside the city of Swansea, in south Wales.

Villages also change over time. Old buildings, such as barns and chapels, are often turned into homes. Villages that are close to towns and cities are very popular. New housing developments are built there. Tea rooms and cafés are set up in some villages to attract **tourists**.

Villages with new developments are becoming larger. Ticehurst in East Sussex is now home to nearly 4,000 people.

In the last few years, some village shops have closed down. Today, most people own a car. They can drive to out-of-town supermarkets and retail parks. Many small villages have lost other services such as banks, post offices and buses. In some places, village schools have closed down, too.

Some villages are popular with tourists. Here, gift shops and cafés do lots of business.

Beddgelert, Snowdonia

Map of the UK

Here are the places mentioned in this book.

KEY
● Villages
● Towns
● Cities

Glasgow ●
● Edinburgh
Jedburgh ●

Belfast ●

Chapel Stile ●

Knaresborough ● ● York
Warrington ●
Liverpool ● ● Manchester
Runcorn ● ● Sheffield
Beddgelert ● ● Newark-on-Trent
● Ashover
Telford ●
● Birmingham
Weobley ● Northampton ● ● Milton Keynes
● Stevenage
St Davids ● ● Finchingfield
● Cirencester
Swansea ● Cardiff ● ● London
● Bristol ● Reading
● Ticehurst
● Corton Denham

Glossary

abandoned deserted and left empty

carnival yearly celebration with music, dancing and other entertainments

cathedral most important church in an area

chain store one of a series of shops selling the same goods

detached not joined to another house

festival organised entertainment event that is held in the same place every year

flats sets of rooms inside a large building

hamlet small village without a church

high street main street with shops in a town

industry business in which a particular product or service is made or sold

inner city area near to the city centre

landmark well-known feature in a town or other landscape

medieval relating to the period between the 5th and 15th centuries

merge join with

new town planned town built to house many thousands of people

pedestrianised closed to vehicles but open to people on foot

pollution damage to the air with dirty and poisonous substances

population number of people who live in a particular place

port town or city where ships can load or unload

regeneration knocking down and rebuilding parts of the town

remote far away from a town or city

retail park group of shops surrounding one large car park

Romans people who lived in and ruled Britain between 27 BC and AD 395

rural relating to the countryside

settlement place set up by a community of people to live in

skyscraper very tall building with many floors

slum overcrowded or poor area of housing

suburbs areas on the edge of a town or city

tourists people who travel for fun

trader person who sells goods

tram vehicle that runs on rails and is powered by electrical cables overhead

university place where students aged 18 or over study

Find out more

Books

Cities, Towns and Villages (Mapping Britain's Landscape), Barbara Taylor (Franklin Watts, 2012)

Mapping a Village, Jen Green (Wayland, 2016)

Population and Settlement (Geographics), Izzi Howell (Franklin Watts, 2017)

Websites

www.bbc.co.uk/schools/gcsebitesize/geography/urban_environments
Urban Environments: *Find out about life in the city.*

www.ordnancesurvey.co.uk/education/index.html
Ordnance Survey Education Resources: *Become a mapping expert with these games and quizzes.*

Index